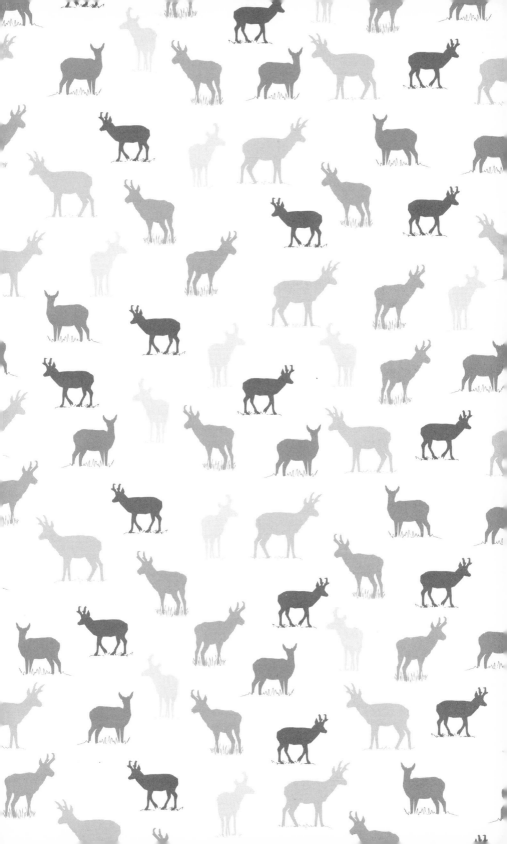

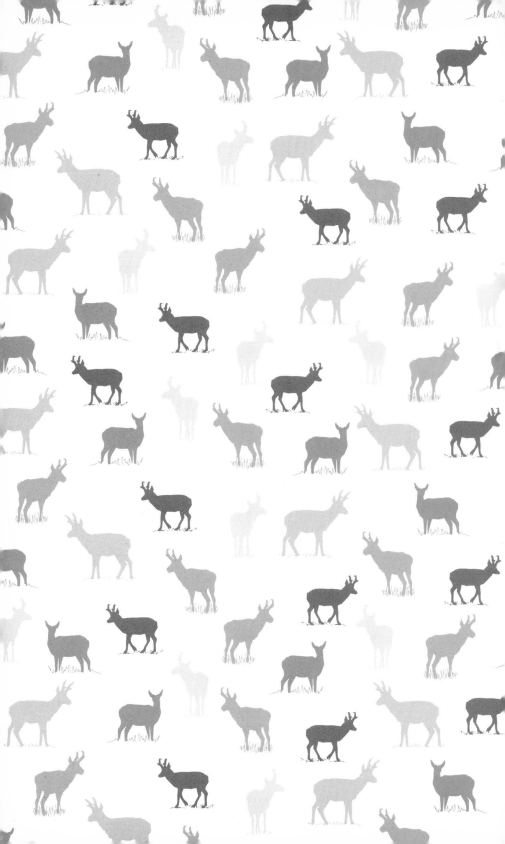

PERRY

A PRONGHORN ANTELOPE

by Bonnie Highsmith Taylor

Perfection Learning®

Cover Photo: Steven Holt—StockPix.com
Photographs courtesy of Jeff Foott: pp. 6, 9, 10, 11, 14, 15,
16, 17, 20, 22, 29, 32, 33, 34–35, 37, 38, 44, 47, 48, 53
Photograph courtesy of Steven Holt—StockPix.com: p. 19
Some images copyright www.arttoday.com
Book Design: Randy Messer & Jan Michalson

Dedication

For the Lebanon Public Library staff

About the Author

Bonnie Highsmith Taylor is a native Oregonian. She loves
camping in the Oregon mountains and watching birds and
other wildlife. Writing is Ms. Taylor's first love. But she also
enjoys going to plays and concerts, collecting antique dolls,
and listening to good music.

Paperback 0-7891-2838-1
Cover Craft® 0-7807-9004-9

CHAPTER

It was a warm sunny morning in May. Spring flowers were blooming. A soft wind blew through the green prairie grass.

A herd of pronghorn antelope grazed on the slope of a hill. There were about 30 pronghorns in the herd. Young bucks and does made up the herd. An older buck was the leader.

One of the does stopped grazing. She seemed nervous. She walked around and around. She shook her head. When another doe came close to her, she butted it.

At last, the doe left the herd. It was time for her to have her fawns. She had to look for a good safe place.

Last fall, she had mated with the leader of the herd. Several other does had also mated with the older buck.

The doe wandered a quarter of a mile away from the herd. She stopped several times. She looked all around. Was it safe? Were there any coyotes around?

Finally, she stopped in a low place. The grass was tall. It was between two small mounds of earth.

She looked all around once more. This would be a good place.

Nearly an hour later, Perry was born. He weighed about six pounds. He was not spotted as baby deer are.

His mother licked him dry. Then she pushed at him with her nose. She made a low bleating sound. She seemed to say "Get up."

Perry got to his feet. He wobbled a little. Then he walked a few steps.

By the time Perry was five or six days old, he would be able to run 20 miles an hour. When he was grown, he would be able to run up to 60 miles an hour.

But for now, he had to lie still in the tall grass. His mother pushed down on his back. Perry lay down.

She nuzzled him with her nose. Perry sniffed his mother. He would remember her smell.

Then the doe left Perry alone. About 100 yards away, she gave birth to another fawn. It was Perry's twin sister. She weighed a pound less than Perry.

Does often drop their fawns some distance apart. Then if a coyote or bobcat finds one fawn, there will still be one left.

It was some time before Perry saw his sister.

For the first few days, the fawns lay very still in the tall grass. An eagle flying overhead could spot a moving fawn. It could carry it off in its long, sharp claws.

The doe came to nurse the fawns often. She would clean them with her long, rough tongue. She would let them walk around a little. Before she left, she would make them lie back down.

Day after day, Perry lay very still. He looked around with his big round eyes. Small animals moved about.

Perry watched a small brown rabbit hopping by. He saw a Western Kingbird carrying bits of dry grass. She was building a nest.

A soft breeze blew over Perry. But Perry had no scent. Other animals could not smell him.

Once a coyote walked nearby. Perry froze. His heart pounded. He held his breath. He knew it was something to fear. He wished his mother was there.

The coyote raised its nose in the air. It sniffed. Then it loped away in search of food.

Perry relaxed. He was safe for now.

CHAPTER 2

Perry and his sister were nine days old. Now they were old enough to join the herd with their mother.

There were several other fawns in the herd. They were the same age as Perry and his sister. The fawns had fun playing together.

They butted heads. They ran around in circles. They kicked up their hind legs.

The other pronghorns in the herd played too. The yearling males were especially playful. They played a little rougher than the fawns.

The leader of the herd was Perry's
father. He seldom played. He usually
stood guard. Sometimes he would
stand away from the herd.

Pronghorns are curious animals.
Anything that moves will draw their
attention.

Pronghorns have excellent vision. Their eyes are very large. They are far apart. This gives them a wide angle of vision. They can see a movement up to four miles away.

They are easily scared. When the leader of the herd spots danger, he warns the others.

A pronghorn has a large patch of long white hairs on its rump. These hairs are longer than other body hair. When a pronghorn is frightened, the stiff, white hairs stand straight up.

The pronghorn can raise and lower the hair very fast. This is a signal. It means danger. And it can be seen up to two miles away.

Perry's father stood about three feet high at the shoulder. He weighed about 125 pounds.

His mother weighed less. She weighed about 85 pounds.

Perry's father was deep tan with white underneath. He had black patches on his cheeks. They looked like sideburns.

His horns were 15 inches long. They were black and shiny. Short prongs grew on the horns. The prongs grew out and slightly upward. This is why they are called *pronghorns.*

Perry's mother did not have black patches on her cheeks. But she had horns. Only they did not have prongs. Her horns were about three inches long. Some does do not have horns.

Every winter, pronghorns shed their horns. They are the only animals in the world that shed horns. Deer shed their antlers. But antlers are not the same as horns.

A short core is left when the horns fall off. By midsummer a new cover grows back over the core. The cover is called a *sheath.*

Pronghorns have been here for over a million years. They have changed very little from their prehistoric ancestors.

Pronghorns are also called American antelope. But pronghorns are not related to the antelope. They are not related to any other animal. They have no close relatives.

Their scientific name means antelope-goat. In some ways, they are like goats and sheep. And in some ways they look like the true antelope.

But true antelope are found only in Asia and Africa. Antelope do not have branched horns. Their horns can be straight or curved. And they do not shed them.

Perry frisked about for a long time with the other fawns. He grew tired. He and his sister nursed. Then they lay side by side and napped.

Their mother grazed nearby.
Some of the other pronghorns
grazed. Others napped. Some just lay
down, staring across the vast prairie.

CHAPTER

Perry grew fast. Life was good. His mother fed and cared for him. He had other fawns to play with.

He was learning about the plants that grew on the prairie. Dandelions, sunflowers, and green grass were good to eat.

Pronghorns can eat things like larkspur, loco weed, yucca, and snakeweed. They even eat cockleburs. These plants are harmful to most animals that graze.

Prairie plants are moist in spring and early summer. So a pronghorn does not need to drink water.

Pronghorns have stomachs with four parts. So do deer and cattle.

Their food goes into the first part. Then it is burped up. It is chewed on for a long time. The lump of food is called a *cud*. The cud is swallowed. It goes through all the parts of the stomach. After a few hours, it is digested.

As summer drew near, the days were getting hotter. The herd scattered in small groups. Perry and his sister and mother roamed with a small group of other does and fawns. The males grouped together. Perry would join this group next year.

Pronghorns usually live where there are not many trees. But they can stand a lot of heat.

They can make their long hair move up and down. They do this by tightening their muscles and then relaxing them. It ruffles the hair. This cools their bodies.

Perry loved the hot summer days. He loved romping over the endless prairie. He loved playing with his sister and the other fawns.

One day, Perry and his sister were playing in the tall grass. Their mother was lying under a juniper tree.

A jackrabbit hopped by. What was this thing? Perry wondered. Did it want to play?

The jackrabbit stopped. It looked at Perry. It twitched its nose. It flicked its long ears.

Perry was sure it wanted to play. He went closer. So did his sister. The rabbit hopped away.

Perry and his sister followed.

They had gone a long way from the rest of the herd.

Suddenly, a coyote came over the hill. Perry and his sister knew coyotes meant danger.

The coyote crouched. He sprang toward the fawns. But Perry's mother appeared. She was ready to protect her young.

The coyote circled the doe. Perry and his sister watched wide-eyed.

The doe struck at the coyote with her sharp front hooves. He dodged them. Again she struck. This time she caught him on the nose.

The coyote shook his head. Then he turned and crawled into the sagebrush.

The two fawns followed their mother back to the herd. The doe started grazing. She acted like nothing had happened.

Warding off coyotes is common. There are many coyotes where pronghorns live. A pronghorn can outrun a coyote if it has to. A pronghorn is the fastest animal in North America. And it is one of the fastest in the world.

But often a pronghorn can stop a coyote by using its horns or its sharp hooves.

Coyotes will turn away unless they

are very hungry. And sometimes the pronghorn is too young to defend itself.

Cougars, bobcats, and coyotes are enemies of the pronghorn. But a pronghorn can outrun them.

A pronghorn's worst enemy is humans. American Indians once hunted pronghorns for food. The hunters would hide in brush or behind a rock. They would wave a tuft of feathers on a long stick. The curious pronghorn would come close enough to be shot with an arrow.

Later, white hunters used this trick. They would tie a rag to a long stick. It was called *flagging*. Now there is a law against flagging.

Pronghorns were native to the prairie. They did not destroy it.

But in the late 1800s, farms sprang up in the West. Cattle grazed on the pronghorns' feeding grounds. They ate most of the grass. They trampled the ground.

As time passed, much of the soil was destroyed. Parts of the country turned into dust bowls.

The early settlers killed thousands of pronghorns. They were in danger of disappearing, just as the buffalo did.

Only a few thousand pronghorns were left by 1908. Once, there had been as many as 100 million.

At last, laws were passed to protect the pronghorns. Now they can only be hunted in season.

CHAPTER 4

It was late August. Hunting season had arrived!

Day after day, guns could be heard. The pronghorns moved farther from the roads.

Several young bucks were killed. These young bucks were from Perry's father's group.

Perry and his sister stayed close to their mother. All the animals were nervous.

Perry was scared by the sounds of guns. He was more frightened than he was by the sound of howling coyotes.

Then one day, Perry saw something in the distance. It was something he had never seen before. Humans! Hunters carrying guns!

He didn't like what he saw. It was something he didn't understand. He could tell his mother was upset. That made him upset too.

Perry did not feel safe even though his mother was near. He had always felt safe before.

Life had changed. It was quiet and peaceful only at night. Sure, coyotes howled and owls hooted. But those were sounds Perry was used to. They did not bother him unless they were very close.

Then one day, the sound of the guns stopped. Hunting season was over!

Once more, Perry and the young pronghorns romped on the prairie.

Perry knew he must always watch for danger. It was part of a pronghorn's life. He was safe for now. But only as long as he was young and healthy. And he had to stay alert at all times.

Coyotes kill pronghorns that are old, weak, or sick. This is nature's way of keeping the herds healthy.

Coyotes also eat a lot of rabbits and ground squirrels. They are easier to catch than pronghorns.

Coyotes can run 30 to 40 miles per hour. Pronghorns have been clocked at nearly 70 miles an hour for short distances. Their speed for long distances is about 40 miles an hour.

A pronghorn's lungs and windpipe are very large. Its heart is twice as big as other animals its size.

A pronghorn runs with its mouth open. This way it gets all the oxygen it can.

Pronghorns live in open areas. They depend on speed and their sharp eyesight.

Perry and his small group moved often. They were always looking for new feeding areas.

One day, they had to cross a river. Perry found out he could swim. Pronghorns are good swimmers.

In the new place, Perry tasted plants he had not tasted before.

Forbs are herbs other than grass. Prairie flowers are forbs. Cornflower, prairie clover, red mallow, and goldenrod are too. There are many others.

They are important in a pronghorn's diet. This is especially true for a doe. It helps her give birth to healthy fawns.

Pronghorns who live in deserts eat cactus plants. They have no trouble eating the sharp needles.

In the spring and summer, they eat a lot of grass and forbs. In the winter, they eat shrubs, mostly sagebrush.

Pronghorns' teeth are strong. They wear down from eating rough plants. But they never stop growing.

Perry loved the sweet, juicy plants along the river. He and the other fawns even fought over them. They would butt one another with their hard heads.

Pronghorns like to feed in farmers' fields. They usually feed there after dark. They also feed in pastures with cattle and horses.

The pronghorns can be hurt jumping fences. So they usually crawl under the bottom wire. In places where there are lots of pronghorns, farmers must keep the lowest wire high above the ground.

Where Perry lived, there were no farms. But there were fences. Cattle grazed on the prairie in the summer. Cattle ranchers put up fences to keep their cattle in. The fences also keep them from mixing with other herds of cattle.

The ranchers kept the bottom wire up high enough for pronghorns to crawl under. Perry learned to crawl under fences at an early age. He learned from his mother and the other pronghorns.

Perry learned a lot of things by watching his mother. She taught him how to survive on the prairie.

CHAPTER 5

By early October, Perry's father and the other bucks had joined the small group. All the small groups came together.

It was mating season. What a lot of banging of horns! And snorting!

Perry looked on in wonder. He and the other fawns tried to stay away from the big bucks and their sharp horns.

About a month after breeding season, the pronghorns would lose their horn covers. Only the bone plugs would be left on their heads. Mice, squirrels, and rabbits would find the old horns. They would chew on them to get minerals.

The new horn covers would start growing right away. By summer, they would be fully grown.

Next fall, Perry would be old enough to breed. But he might have to wait.

The older bucks fight the younger ones to keep them away from the does. So many bucks are not able to breed for three or four years.

Next fall, Perry's sister would breed. She would have a fawn in the spring. Does usually have only one fawn the first time.

The days were still warm and sunny on the prairie. There was still lots of good food.

Perry found plenty to do. Besides eating, he spent hours playing with all the other fawns.

And he spent a lot of time exploring. Like most young animals, he was curious.

One day, Perry wandered away from the herd. He went all alone. He found a low-growing shrub with tasty leaves. For a while, he feasted.

When a sage grouse appeared, he followed it. It disappeared into a thicket of silverberry.

Something else caught Perry's attention. Dirt was flying in the air. Perry went closer. Clods of dirt hit him.

From a wide hole, Perry could see a short tail. Hind legs were kicking up dirt.

What could this be? Perry wondered. And what was it doing?

The animal was an old badger. It turned around. When it saw Perry, it snarled. For a moment, Perry froze. He was surprised. He had never seen a badger before.

It didn't look like an animal Perry would like. And it didn't look like it wanted to play.

The badger snarled again. It hissed. At first, Perry thought about striking at it with his front hooves. That was what his mother had done. Once he had seen her strike at a bobcat. The bobcat had turned and run away.

But Perry decided to do what the bobcat had done. He turned and ran all the way back to the herd.

His mother and sister were napping. Perry decided that was a good idea. He lay down nearby and went to sleep. He had explored enough for one day.

Before the summer and fall ended, Perry had met a lot of other prairie animals.

Once, he was chased by an angry cow. All Perry wanted to do was smell the newborn calf.

Another time, he was pecked on the rump by an unfriendly sandhill crane. He had been grazing too close to it.

And there was the time he was sprayed by a skunk for no reason at all.

Luckily, the skunk wasn't close. So only a little spray touched Perry. But it was a smell that he did not like.

Perry learned a good lesson. Don't mess with angry cows, unfriendly cranes, and especially skunks.

CHAPTER

It was snowing! Perry had never seen snow before. He wasn't sure if he liked it. The cold didn't bother him. His coat kept him warm.

The long outer hairs of a pronghorn's coat are hollow. They fill with air. The hairs flatten against the animal's body. This holds in the warmth.

It was quieter on the prairie now except for the howling of the wind. And the wind never stopped blowing.

There were no birds singing. They were all gone. They had gone where it was warmer.

Many small animals had gone into holes in the ground. Some were hibernating. Others were waiting out the winter. Snakes had denned together through the cold months.

There were still jackrabbits hopping around.

Coyotes and bobcats were about. They have to hunt for food all year round. They eat a lot of mice in the winter.

Mice move under the snow. Coyotes and bobcats can hear them even through the snow. They dig them out and eat them.

The snow was not very deep yet. Perry and the other pronghorns could scratch through it. They ate the grass underneath.

But early one morning, the sky turned dark gray. The wind blew harder and harder. It was time to leave the low prairie.

Perry moved with the herd to their winter feeding place. It was up very high. Here the wind blew harder. The hard winds blew the snow from sagebrush.

The pronghorns depended on the sagebrush for their winter food. Also, there were rock canyons up high. These were good shelters from the icy cold.

Perry would need to hunt for food all winter. Pronghorns do not build up fat. They need the same amount of food all year.

In the winter, all the pronghorn groups come together. Often there are over 100 pronghorns in a herd.

The winter was hard and long and very cold. Many animals did not make it. Coyotes hunted in packs when the snow was deep. They killed some of the older and weaker pronghorns. Only the strongest of the herd survived the hard winter.

Perry thought the cold would never end. How he missed the warm sunny days. He missed romping with the other fawns on the prairie. There was no time for play. The only important thing was food and shelter.

Sometimes Perry would hear the screams of cougars in the night. It was a frightening sound. As frightening as the sound of the guns he had heard last summer.

Perry was still not grown. He would not reach full size until he was about 16 months old.

At last, the snow began to melt. There were some days that were warm. By the first of April, the herd moved down to the low prairie. The does were heavy with fawns. In a few weeks, they would be born.

New life was all over the prairie. Baby animals were being born in burrows—skunks, ground squirrels, badgers, and rabbits.

In fox dens, newborn puppies squirmed and nursed. Soon the playful pups would tumble out of the den.

Some birds were returning. Perry saw meadowlarks, blackbirds, killdeer, and bob-o-links.

Perry loved being back on the prairie. He loved running as fast as he wanted to. He loved the warm sun and the new grasses that were sprouting. They tasted so good, especially after months of only sagebrush.

In May, Perry's mother gave birth to two more fawns. Perry had a new brother and sister.

The large herd formed smaller groups for the summer. This year Perry was in a group of yearlings and two-year-old males. This is called a *bachelor herd.*

Perry and the other young bucks fought among themselves. It was mostly in play. But it was also practice. Someday they would be leaders of their own herds.

By early summer, young animals were everywhere. Baby birds had hatched. Some had already left their nests.

Perry's new siblings were romping with other fawns. He and his sister had done just that last summer.

There were many sweet, juicy plants to eat. The grass was tall and green. It was a good time to be alive living on the wild and wide-open prairie. It was a good time for a pronghorn antelope.

CHAPTER

Pronghorns have suffered because of humans. Many animals have. But luckily, some people fight for animals' needs and rights.

Ernest Thompson Seton was a man who studied wild animals. He felt bad about what people had done to the buffalo. And he felt bad about what they were doing to the pronghorn and other wildlife.

He wrote books about it. People read his books. They knew he was right. Wildlife should be saved. Too many animals were becoming endangered. Many were extinct.

National parks and refuges were built. In these places, wildlife could live safe from humans.

Yellowstone is the biggest and oldest national park in America. Many pronghorns live there.

In Oregon, thousands of pronghorns live on Hart Mountain National Antelope Refuge. There are refuges in several other states.

In 1983 in Wyoming, 1,000 pronghorns starved to death. They could not reach their winter feeding place.

A farmer had built a tight fence around thousands of acres. The fence stretched 28 miles. It blocked the pronghorns' way to their winter feeding area.

When people found out about the fence, they were angry. The National Wildlife Federation and other conservationists took the farmer to court. He was ordered to tear down the fence.

The farmer tried to fight the order. He tried to take the case to the Supreme Court. The Supreme Court refused to listen to the case. The fence had to come down.

Once again, the huge herds of pronghorns could migrate to their winter feeding places.

Animals' rights had won over people's rights.

For more information, contact

Pronghorn National Wildlife Refuge

1776 Massachusetts Ave., NW Suite 200

Washington, D.C. 20036

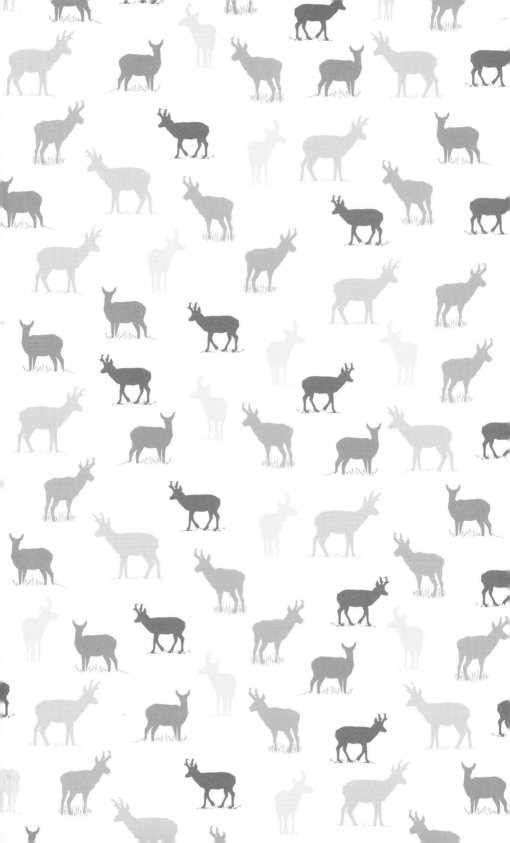